For Jill, my fabulous 'farm girl' friend,
with love

CRASH, BANG, THUD!
by Dawn Apperley

British Library Cataloguing in Publication Data
A catalogue record of this book is available from the British Library.

ISBN 0 340 78800 3 (HB)
ISBN 0 340 78801 1 (PB)

First edition published 2001
10 9 8 7 6 5 4 3 2

Published by Hodder Children's Books,
a division of Hodder Headline Limited,
338 Euston Road, London NW1 3BH

Printed in Hong Kong

CRASH, BANG, THUD!

A Noisy Story About Being Quiet

by Dawn Apperley

Hodder Children's Books

A division of Hodder Headline Limited

Mr Macdonald was a farmer, who liked things quiet.
He lived on his peaceful farm with just one dozy dog called Dez.

One day was much like the next for
Mr Macdonald and Dez, until . . .

. . . two crazy cows congaed up to the farm.
'Cool farm,' they mooed. 'Can we live here?'

'If you promise to be very quiet,' Mr Macdonald said.
So, on his farm he had one dog and two cows.

Then three playful pigs trotted by the farm.
'Nice place,' they oinked. 'Can we live here?'
'If you keep the noise down,' whispered Mr Macdonald.
So, on his farm he had one dog, two cows and three pigs.

Then four silly sheep skipped up to the farm.
'Fab farm,' they baaed. 'Can we live here?'
'If you promise not to riot and rampage,'
muttered Mr Macdonald.

So, on his farm he had
one dog,
two cows,
three pigs
and four sheep.

Then five rabbits, six hens, seven ducks and eight bees
all arrived at Mr Macdonald's farm.

'Great farm!' they shouted. 'Can we live here?'

Mr Macdonald found it fun having one dog, two cows, three pigs, four sheep, five rabbits, six hens, seven ducks, eight bees and nine butterflies – who fluttered by and stayed – on his farm.

For a while everyone was very, very quiet, but then...

ink

quack

Moo

baa

Oink

Buzz

Everyone forgot to be even
a little bit quiet, especially Dez!

Mr Macdonald's farm was NOISY!

'**W**hatever shall I do?' wondered Mr Macdonald.

Then he had an idea and got to work.

This time, it was Mr Macdonald who made
all the noise!

Mr Macdonald made a special home for everyone . . .

...and everyone was

happy.

But then . . .

...ten space ships detected Mr MacDonald's farm!
'Ummm, nice farm,' bleeped one hundred
chattering aliens, all looking for a place to live!